C000303084

THE HEARING ROOM

THE HEARING ROOM

Hubert Moore

Shoestring Press

All rights reserved. No part of this work covered by the copyright
hereon may be reproduced or used in any form by any means –
graphic, electronic, or mechanical, including copying, recording, taping,
or information storage and retrieval systems – without written
permission of the publisher.

Typeset and printed by Q3 Print Project Management Ltd,
Loughborough, Leics
(01509) 213456

Published by Shoestring Press
19 Devonshire Avenue, Beeston, Nottingham, NG9 1BS
(0115) 925 1827
www.shoestringpress.co.uk
First published 2006
© Copyright: Hubert Moore
The moral right of the author has been asserted.
ISBN-13: 978 1 904886 33 4
ISBN-10: 1 904886 33 7

Shoestring Press gratefully acknowledges financial assistance from
Arts Council England

ACKNOWLEDGMENTS

Thanks are due to the editors of: Connections, Dream Catcher, Equinox, The Independent, The Interpreter's House, Magma, Modern Poetry in Translation, The North, Other Poetry, Oxford Magazine, Rialto and The New Writer, in whose Poetry Collection Competition (2003) ten of these poems, under the title 'Whoever', won second prize.

*This collection is dedicated to victims of torture everywhere,
particularly to members of the Medical Foundation
Write-to-Life group, with whom I have been privileged to work
and grieve and laugh.*

CONTENTS

I

Translation   3
How to listen   4
Tennis with Haydn   5
Music   6
In Mongolia   7
Newport away   8
Orange   9
Onion   10
At a loss   11
Dead-heading   12
Absence   13
For Mack Mehrabian, baker   14
Deep Third Man   15
The Good Asker   16
Carnation   18
Approaching Reading   19
Welcome to Marden   20
Turning   22
Act of betrayal   23
At the cricket   24
Visitant   25
The Singing Lesson   26
I.D.   28

II

Dear Fahimeh   31
In the Hearing Room   33
At the house of my father (1–5)   34
Notice of arrival   39
Three   40
Colouring in   41
Telling the road   42
On the border path   43
Picnic   44
On the English train   45
Prisoners   46

Ash   47
November 5th   48
Dream warfare   49
Locked   50
Asylum   51
The burning house (1–9)   52

I

TRANSLATION

Aujourd'hui
(There is always)

je suis tres content.
(a weir coming up.)

C'est agreable
(The green river)

de recevoir une personne
(streams downstream)

avec qui
(stops)

on peut
(then topples)

sympathiser.
(delightedly over.)

HOW TO LISTEN

With the ears of course, where
every story enters, spirals
in and away.

Not with the nose (though many
do listen that way). The trouble is
our bony convexities can't quite
forget the thought of themselves:
our pernickety nose, our fingers
making their point, our feet in the door.

Listen with the hollows of the body:
the ears, yes, and the eyes and the mouth
and, I recommend, the undersides
of the knees. Is the listener sitting?
Well, under the knees, unseen, concave,
a cradle, that's where the wild-eyed
stories will come, then, next day,
next month, or the next, let
slip, let spout out under the table,
what was done, where, how.

TENNIS WITH HAYDN

My fearful courageous Aunt Violet
took me to hear Haydn.
It was my first, her last time.

I remember tea on the train.
I remember sitting by Violet
when music burst into our heads.

Eighty years unmarried,
for most of those years she had kept,
with her book and her pills and her glasses,

a tennis ball at her bedside.
You never knew with men.
Best to be safe and roll the tennis ball

under the bed before getting in.
And in the early hours,
if she woke and wanted the comfort,

she could roll again and see
the ball come through untouched. Unless
that wasn't floorboards

restless under the bed, but a dense
thing with head and shoulders and knees
that had slept perhaps but now

rolled out and eased its stiffness
and stood in the air
and filled the eyes with its body,

the ears with the oil of its voice:
the 'Oxford', the 'London',
or one of the String Quartets.

MUSIC

Music of tins
by someone like Vivaldi.
You take the wrappings off
and throw them in.

Each tin goes down the same,
goes bouncing empty down
the throat to be
recycled.

Each is a fragment
of a piece, I think, for mandolin
or lute; a phrase plucked
and repeated.

Don't expect a message.
The rhythm that you hear
is of a tin
which doesn't say it once had
rabbit-flavoured cat-food in it,
pilchards, chopped tomatoes, garden peas.

A poem would have loved all this
but tins are different.
They rattle off without nutrition
information, recommended recipes,
words.

Music's as clean as that.

IN MONGOLIA

In the mountains they howled for wolves,
and the local echoes,

on the spur (echoes use this term
to stand for inspiration),

dashed off a noise to go
across the awful chasms

of the mute, the unspeakable,
to where the howls had come from.

From cliff to cliff it banged,
blank, inarticulate,

yet when it came was
an answer, phrased, precise:

half wolfishness,
half serious human laughter.

NEWPORT AWAY

Newport's still there then, first stop
after the Severn, no distance now, a sleep
and a coffee-and-croissant from Paddington.

My friend went. Checked out the shopping,
found in some winsome glitterhouse
a jumper stylish as London or Italy.

Not like the old days. Not like Rodney Parade –

where, every October in the 1950s and 60s,
we lightweight London nancy-boys went cheerfully
to defeat. The mist was in place before us,
the home soil licked its lips: we squelched
as we ran, while the Black-and-Ambers
bulldozed through or tip-toed over the top of it.

Mining men on weekdays, their locks, their pit-props.
We could hardly embrace some of them, let alone
tackle. We were brave of course, we had style,
our haughty side-steppers glittered a little,
long white legs in the mist. We scored once or twice.

Newport, though, they ran through us for their lives,
for their aunts and uncles, for their fathers who scored
before them, for their girls from up on the terraces.
Touching down was touching down in the valley.

Most of it's gone, though even now I can hear
a spring-heeled Newport voice dancing clear
of the clogged throat of the system:
"Ken Jones scored the try; Brian Jones converted."

Beyond that, nothing: we set off for London
so smoothly we don't even move. There are light
refreshments available, the old days
are gliding west and throughout the train
there's a policy of no smoking.

ORANGE

We drove through the dust
of the high flat land between cities
to where Africa slopes to sea.

In the red gusts
a storm broke open across us
and puddles filled with angry orangey

rain. For a whole blue day
no mention was made of this, there was
no tomorrow, yesterday

never took place. Next morning,
out where the fathoms get serious,
as far as the eye

could guess there was endless blue.
Near though, in the shallows,
muddied orange was steadily

making waves. All that day
orange rose from its wrinkles,
rocked in the arms of the bay.

ONION

On your first visit
to fond new widower me,
you brought a beautiful dark-red onion.

Onions don't mean a thing.
Their multi-layers aren't layers of memory
(the more you peel, the more tearful).

Onions are themselves.
Yours sits here on the table
broad-bottom-heavy, a dark red globe of its own.

And yet how uxorious onions are
in a dish. They'll marry with anything,
steak, vegetables, cheese.

I must still have that recipe somewhere:
red onion and apple,
poems and the people who write them.

AT A LOSS

I am your grief. When I first
came to you, I had no words.
All I could utter was a sort
of roaring curse.

I came to stay of course.
I think you thought I'd howl myself
and go. You had language though,
I copied it

and made my howls articulate.
"Speak me," I learnt to say, "make
mention of me, mutter me
in your sleep." All

this you did for me but still
my rawness pleaded: "Thread me
through you, let me come between
your things and you."

Slipping you on I grew
a body where I watched my slow
wound raise its sides and inch towards
a healing. I

was something now, I'd occupy
the air, fill up a pocket of it,
have an edge, an end. I might be
your live-in lover

the way you mind me, hoover
round the space you know I need.
Trust me, dear griever, I'm complete
and commonplace,

I promise.

DEAD-HEADING

('But rather look thy sorrow mightily in the face')

It's sad when dead-heading comes round,
especially of daffodils.

It's not so sad for them. If we
were daffodils we'd always be thinking,
'This year we've done OK. We did our best
to make the spring a feast. Next year, next existence,
so long as we get dead-headed,
we'll do even better.'

We'd be quite happy as daffodils.
We could yearn, we could strive, we could shine,
we could tell each other of somewhere else
to progress to.

And what would daffodils think
if they were us?
They'd stare down their trumpets,
give us their whole pale gaze.
They'd think of nothing but the withering
of men's wonderful heads.

Dead-heading us would be all they had in mind.

ABSENCE

You are not here and absence
is frisky without you. It's only
the wind, no doubt, that whisks
rigid the haunches and hurls
the rag-cat body of absence

sheer up the trunk of a tree.
Claws ripping at bark-flesh, is
this what I've made of absence?
This wired-up tail-dance? This
mad stare down through leaves?

Or absence immaculate,
every limb licked, every outcry
absorbed in the ribbed blur
of its sleeping: a slick of oil
poured into luxury's lap?

FOR MACK MEHRABIAN, BAKER

When I told you about my wife,
you gave me a loaf,
straight off,

out of the crate
you were carrying, out of what
must be your fullness of heart, a state

of constant readiness,
blood always coursing, I guess,
always on the *qui vive* – in case

someone perhaps whose wife is dead
comes by, whose crying need
is for bread

or for something that's risen or rises.

DEEP THIRD MAN

(Poem for a retired wicket-keeper)

That leg-side stumping of yours
hangs safe in the memory
(if not of the man you stumped).

But then you said that the bowler
who started the incident off
was a medium-paced

maths teacher, who would never
leap to conclusions nearly
as quick as yours,

but kept to a length, I guess,
and showed his workings, how he got
wherever he got,

then went to deep third man.

THE GOOD ASKER

Younger brothers have to go and spend.
This one takes his portion, gathers
all together as the text requires
and goes.

The elder brother seems to me
to feel this weightily: he goes
nowhere, his substance on his back.
Of course the younger one is due
to waste all his, get poor,
get hungry, get regretful
and come home.

Before he makes it though, his father's
senses rise and tell him where
his son is coming from and so
he runs the best run of his life
or anyone's to where the boy
is penitent and still far off.

Back home the father needs a time
to tell the servants who to lay for,
what to serve, and while he's busy,
I'd make, off the record and in
envy almost, the elder son
the patron saint of asking

if when the brothers meet again
outside the text, maybe inside
the byre where the calf has fattened,
he isn't rough, he doesn't punch

the prodigal, but because he lets
his mind prick up inside him
he asks his brother:

"Brother, is the city wonderful?
Are you different now? When you're
with harlots, can it seem they really
love you? What's it like to spend?"

CARNATION

Of all the supergoods
the customer in front of me
had nothing but a bunch
of red carnations
to lay before the check-out.

How many flowers you get
per bunch I couldn't see. I
wanted her to turn and say
that since she'd been a mother
of the disappeared in Istanbul

one red carnation was all
she had in mind. At which
I wanted me to ask her
in Turkish if I spoke it,
Was it worse than grief

the never knowing if
there's hope your son is locked
in somewhere low and narrow
each day getting narrower
or he's dead? Also,

if you never know,
can you hold up for ever
his absence, his single stem
of dark red disappearance,
between the thumb and forefinger

and keep erect your anger?

APPROACHING READING

'This train will surely be arriving
at Reading.' And we've been moving

so sweetly along our line,
so single-mindedly. Acton

glided past as though it had
to happen, then Slough, then Maidenhead:

Reading we thought a natural
consummation, until

this First Great Western man
loudspoke himself uncertain.

Without at least a glottal stop,
God might have given up:

no signalling system, no word,
no getting anywhere.

WELCOME TO MARDEN

"The difficulty is not that of finding the solution but rather that of recognizing as the solution something that looks as if it were only the preliminary to it." (Wittgenstein)

The Ramsgate train, the last one
out from London, Saturday night,
has just announced that Staplehurst –

my start, my end, where going's first
excited cries come echoing
back, where I loop my loop –

is our next station-stop.
It's not. Next stop's a pocket
of wet night, not Staplehurst at all,

not its width of platform, not its style
of bridge, yet when the guard insists,
"Get off or don't get off. This station's

Staplehurst," I drop the difference
and watch my train set off for what's
announced as Ramsgate: settle

for quiet, stillness, half-lit drizzle
and a notice on the platform
opposite: "Welcome to Marden" –

which has a hut to shelter in,
a narrow tip-up ledge for sitting
down on and a sense of it

being mildly possible to wait
for half an hour or ever
on the platform. All down the line,

although a fiery glow of non-
co-operation goes from stop
to thwarted stop, soon all's

amended: Ashford International's
nothing but the one-hut stop
before it, Folkestone Central's

merely Folkestone West, Deal's
Walmer, and Ramsgate, much announced
as end, conclusion, terminus,

is preliminary Sandwich, place
of passage, where people, streets and squares
are all describable and that's

TURNING

I chose the turn-off to the roundabout.

I could, could still, have indicated right
and stood there winking till a saint
among those driving down the straight and narrow
flashes and lets me in.

I don't quite do this,
though the straight-ahead proceeders
seem saintly enough: my near-right-mindedness
I'm sure they'd recognize

though what I do
is not insinuate myself within their corridor
of light, their inching homewards one
behind the scarcely fuming other,

but turn off left
towards the roundabout and enter
such a point-blank agitated contraflow
of all the cars and little vans

that streetniks drive, and slipper-men, sock-walkers,
tea-ists, askers, natural-cyclists, bed-adherents,
tinklers, absent-minders, heart-men, joiners,
listening-artistes,

that all their exits block,
although beyond the exits, lit and radiant,
are their streets, kindly abbreviations
of the saints they are.

ACT OF BETRAYAL

Wartime, the 1940s, and the only light
in tight-lipped, blackouted Britain
was a steady yellow blink from across our valley
where the top of the hill would be.

My brother said he knew the code, he could read it,
there were Germans up there signalling.
Now was the time to free ourselves, they were saying,
to betray. There must be thousands of us.

Auntie Connie said we were seeing things.
'Oxford ideas', that's what she said we'd got.
I think she thought we'd gone queer in the head down south.
She was north – my father used to say 'Antie'.

Sixty years later I climbed the hill to see.
Auntie Connie was right, there's nothing there:
only gorse, gold as you like, and a rich crop of stone.
No sign of a lonely man with a torch;
a discarded battery, chicken bones, a waterlogged fire.

That night I checked: watched from the front room
of the B and B with the curtains drawn back.
Nothing, then something. Across the valley
they must have seen me, sitting here in the dark.
"Calling all traitors": I found I knew the code.

AT THE CRICKET

Kent are playing Lancashire today.
We are interested to see what happens.

My neighbour says it's thick as shit, the atmosphere.
He says, You watch, it'll swing a mile.

A train goes by beyond the rhododendrons.
It gives two hoots. Quite near us
a lithe West Indian is deep third man.

We're clustered round a green arena
in a sort of dip. Which must be why
the pleasant summer haze
hangs on and on. It can't get out
and we can't not inhale it.

You should hear our clapping: how,
all round the ground, when someone hurls or hits, ·
we crackle up. Nothing actually catches,
but what if it did?

If the mist cleared and mild-mannered them
rose up and turned on mild-mannered us?
Decent us came out against decent them?

Left versus right I mean,
not Kent v. Lancashire at all.

It's thick as shit, the atmosphere.
It will swing a mile.

VISITANT

Mushtaq Ali, the beautiful
Indian cricketer, is dead.
As a child I think

I once saw him, if not in the flesh.
The obituary says
he was lithe, upright, graceful

as ever at 90. I backed
England of course; felt quite guilty
worshipping foreign gods,

wanting Mushtaq Ali
always to lose and be best.
Like Christ, I suppose, though I doubt

Christ had wrists like Mushtaq Ali's.
I think wristy gods are the best,
ones that can glide

a straight ball down to third man,
or glance it. Not like
thunderbolt hookers and drivers.

THE SINGING LESSON

In the War Memorial Hall
where we spent our peace-time Sunday
learning to sing Bulgarian songs
at the very back of our throats,

a stone tablet commemorates
Lance-Corporal William Cutter
of 2 Barton Cottages in this town,
who won the VC for devotion
to duty and most conspicuous

bravery. We can't get back to the place
where the song comes up from. His
right knee blown off and both arms wounded,
he still had a cheery word for passers-by
in the 14 hours till they stretchered

him back from the line. We have to fetch
machine-guns, our Bulgarian teacher says,
from inside the base of the neck. We stutter
point-blank at each other, vibrato,
high-key, low-key. Cutter

had dragged the last of him to a crater,
where, under fire, he steadied the men
who were holding it. Our teacher says
we must quiver along with it,
let our voices take their power

from the heart. For hours
we hold the position, then when we're almost
back to the aching source of the sound,
almost become Bulgarian,
we split forces, take different parts:

some to leap wherever the spurts
of the song flame us; some
to be drones, to keep the note, to stay
in the same old crater, hardly
hearing discordance, heads down

at 2 Barton Cottages in this town.

ID

A passport will do. Otherwise
all they need is a modest
collection of poems, title and name
on the front, and a face-only
photo of the author himself
looking poetic on the back.

You get through the gate and they frisk you,
strip each poem from the page
and make it stand with its arms out.
They finger the ribbed cage of the lines,
count syllables, check for a rhyme-scheme
strapped to the calf or thigh.

OK, they sigh in the end. Yet again
they've found nothing, certainly not
anger, the small explosive
you flatter yourself you concealed
at the time of writing – to go
decorously off in the white

silences between stanzas.

II

DEAR FAHIMEH

*(The poem, originally in Farsi, is for Fahimeh Taghadosi,
executed in Iran, 1982.*

*The writer is unknown. Farkhondeh Ashena, who recently
escaped from Iran, heard it when she was in solitary confine-
ment, and memorised it. Nasrin Parvaz translated.)*

That day,
that hot day in July,
when the Evin loudspeakers
called out your beautiful name and your lips
smiled, your eyes said to your friends,
'So today is the day.'

You went and your walk
was a perfume filling the corridor.
Everyone gasped, everyone asked with their eyes,
'Is today then the day?' The Pasdar
flung back an answer: 'Where is her bag?
Where are her veil, her socks, her money?'

A rumour went round that you'd given a sign
that yes, today was the day:
'I don't need my food', you had said.

So tonight is the night.
A silence hangs in the heart of it.
Friends look at friends and tell themselves
that perhaps you'll come back.

Fahimeh dear, tell us, spare
a word for your friends. Is
the sky sad where you are, does it weep?
And the wind, does it ruffle your veil?
Back here, the ward sweats for your news.

And a message gets through:
wind-blown breathless dandelion
comes from the mountains to say that clouds
are massing up there and they're big with child.

Head held high, you are standing and waiting for this,
for the clouds to open, for you
to be mother of change.

Rifles crack.
The moorland holds its breath
at a star shooting across it.

It would be good to sing and go with friends
to face the firing squad, to dance,
to float in the rain.

In the long sea-silence,
a wave lifts, oars clip at the water.

A young fisherman bringing his boat to land,
rice-growers trudging home,
they shape their lips to your name.

Your name is beautiful for young girls born in July.

IN THE HEARING ROOM

"There were rebels, you say,
sleeping in the house of your father?"

At the first kick
you hear the cheap timber gasp.

Gendarmerie, guards, officers, enterers, wrenchers.

Even the adjudicator is amongst the men
at the door of your father's house.

The adjudicator is perfectly dressed, perfectly spoken.
You long to please him, tell him the story he wants.
But you can't say. Fear has damaged your head.
Or shame. Or the breaking door.

So how come the man at the back of the court
swells with rebels
sleeping at the house of your father?

He brings them tea, eggs, oranges;
he watches them eat.

AT THE HOUSE OF MY FATHER

1.

In the dim-lit attic dormitory
my father goes from bed to bed,
rebel to rebel. He has dragged up
every cushion, every rug in the house.

These boys are second sons to him.
He tweaks their soft ideals, their tufts,
their downiness; wishes them
good sleep, the sleep of men unwanted.

They drop their limbs like clothes:
take what's on offer
while, through the blur of breathing,
their ears' devices brim with news from the dark.

Last thing, as though I were all rebels,
my father's face leans down and kisses
my smooth one. All evening I've scoured
the rebels' pans with something as prickly.

2.

Mornings I work in the washroom.
Before hanging I put
the rebels' clothes through the mangle.

They come from the sink drowned:
slumped shirts with their arms in the legs
of slumped trousers.

I ease them back into shape,
stretch out the arms in innocence,
make a V of the trousers.

Then, as I put them through,
I watch the men's cold fear
sluicing out down the runnels.

3.

The rebels have one bicycle
between the lot of them.
It has flat tyres and the chain
is a dangling necklace.

But might
rebels not need a bicycle
to ghost off into the night
no one knows where (not
till it comes home pedals in shreds,
spokes gone, arms twisted)?

I can do punctures: hold
the breath under water, wait
for the gash in the inner tube
to show me the place, to come
trumpeting up in bubbles.

I can do chains: upside-down
hand-pedal inches forward
till the racked links take,
the cogs remember.

At the back of my father's house,
the gaunt frame drums its wheels
for when a ghost might need it.

4.

The men found our old kettle
from before the regime.
After that there was no holding them:

our two benches in front of the stove,
they sit inside themselves
and hear in the distance the first

mew and tick of spirits about
to rise, then, in the whisperings
as the chest and shoulders fill,

their sense of justice
wheezes, courage croaks,
purpose breathes up the spout.

5.

Over the rebels' heads,
on my father's rooftop,
I spend clogged grey evenings
sending my pigeons out
on their rounds and calling them.

The hatch clatters back.
Rebels are nothing now, only
a thud of cards; sometimes,
when one of them plays his ace,
a rumble up of men,

a beat of wings. Once
out of their cage, the pigeons
gust free as the thick
air unlocks and lets them
go swirling through it.

The men don't know but they gave
my pigeons their names.
I keep them just under the breath:
no pigeon is mentioned by name
when I call them home.

NOTICE OF ARRIVAL

I am shut in the hold of my head.
It's so dark I'm bodiless
yet I blunder about and bruise
on the luggage I'm stacked with,
memories, fear, loss.

The drivers are up on deck.
For the moment this juggernaut's mine.
We have come all this way together,
its roaring shudder and the shudder
of my muteness. As for its snore
I know it like it must know
the cry, the nakedness of my waking.
Perhaps it can feel at the back of the neck
me wafting amongst its freight.

I'm becoming more pointed, I think, more
ship-shaped as we cross. I'm the tip
of the iceberg, I know, tapered, stream-lined
for parting the water. I can picture
the thin frothed-up wake I leave behind me;

and how hugely we're nosing in
between harbour walls. I have to get
back now into my limbs, re-enter
my rib-cage, put on the empty boots
of my legs, and my old voice-trumpet.

One thing I have decided: when I come,
I shall come clean, quite openly tell them
that I'm almost nobody.

THREE

Today is English numbers.
Today is no problem:
these are only numbers.

Except that three
is how many the neighbours
took to the woods from his family

and hanged. No, the tongue
has to come up and actually
touch the cutting

edge of the teeth. His father
and his mother
and his elder brother.

Like this: "Three."
But the tongue has a root of its own.
Tree. Tree. Tree.

COLOURING IN

Each boy has a blank sheet which is a continent.
Nothing is written, only the outlines of countries,
their home-countries, jagged and distant and sweet.

Their blind man's fingers touch the flat of the map.
They should mark if they can their towns, their villages.
There is a red pencil provided for this.

The atlas shows them how to spell their cities.
They should mark cities in black. Purple is for mountains,
gold for a desert, blue for the sea.

It takes a long quiet time to colour a country.
But already Iraq has ranges of aubergine,
Sri Lanka has a bright blue fringe round it
and Somalia's sand has fountained into the sea.

One of the boys won't have it. He has stopped colouring
and rammed his elbows into the ant-heaps of cities.
'Here is not my country,' he says. His neighbours
lean over to see. He is right. There is nothing there,
and at the moment of colouring he is shading his eyes
against forgetting, against finding his country strange.

TELLING THE ROAD

The story can only be told
when the two travel like this:

the driver locked in his lane,
unwavering, not even glancing,

and the silent, far-fetched passenger
strapped, gazing ahead as the road
hurtles back at him, how
soldiers came to the farm, he can't
say more, his head must have swallowed …

Yet when the two men go like this
down their different lanes, he might
come mildly across the words
on the dotted line in his head,
he might even tell the road

what was done, his voice
leaping and stopping and trembling
over lovely cratered fields.

ON THE BORDER PATH

I take you along this gentle path between counties,
Kent, as it happens, and Sussex. Way
above us and utterly white on blue,
the clouds are a picture: Truth and Justice and Mercy.

Quick, wary, in unsuitably shiny shoes,
you're pleased, I'm sure, this isn't Iran we're skirting;
not quite at ease, though, in all this rolling mildness,
this rich, lucky, carefully planted place.

'There are even now mines in these fields?'
I walk alongside you at the very edge.
In the staccato of your almost excellent English
I can't not hear the quake in the hills of your head:

the border erupting, the grassy lid of it
lifted from under your feet, under your shiny shoes.

PICNIC

You remember our seaside picnic,
what a storm we ran into?
And how we were all flinging wildly,
swatting out of or through.

I was afraid that my white
was what thunder-flies dream of.
But your stripes were the same,
black-spattered, a bug-hive.

Odd you should swat your way
from Zaire to find that asylum
is picking specks off a cold meat pie,
then off strawberries and cream.

We didn't get stung – that was good,
but the best of the picnic was this:
how mildly discomfort thundered,
wanted to be with us, touch us;

and, even more, how it didn't care
that you'd had to flee from torture
and I had not. Here's to discomfort,
its indiscriminate spatter.

ON THE ENGLISH TRAIN

She has her bag on the rack
directly above her head.
Hopefully it won't burst out in the train.

Inside it there are her pictures,
there is a gauzy orange memory of her mother,
there are last-minute thoughts, a jumble.

What she dreads most
is that amid all this mildness,
amid the steady breathing of the English train,

her mind will go off

and everyone will hear
the panting of a police car
through the streets of her horrified city.

PRISONERS

Their affectionate uncle
escaped from prison
and went to prison in England.

He took his torturer with him.

Free over there, he could live,
he could write his articles;
all he had learnt by heart
he could pour into unrhymed lines,
into open-ended stanzas.

If he didn't write,
then his nieces, both newly married,
could lie awake in the early hours
unworried about their doors,
how their quietly altered addresses,
almost unseasoned timber,
at the first kick
would splinter in on them,

and he would still be in prison.

ASH

The play we saw
blazed for more than an hour.
Those nearest it got burnt
in just those places
where burns had occurred before.

On the way home
you pointed out that ash
was what you were:
the left-over of flames, the frothy
settlement of fire-flesh

that you thought had cooled
at last. Till someone in a bus
or theatre or book
stirs it.
Then your dear smoke rises.

NOVEMBER 5TH

The gunshots in your head
go off on Guy Fawkes Night
in north west London, Brent.

The same explosions sent
you spinning back beneath your windows,
running from Africa

to a roadside where
you have to duck your head
again and see again

the body of your broken-
headed neighbour trampled
as you run. It's

Guy Fawkes Night and gunshots
whine and crack at you
in Africa, in Brent.

DREAM WARFARE

I think torturers don't so much dream
as make sudden dream appearances,
and the terrible tapes unwind night after night
in Toronto and Stockholm and Birmingham.
You'd think they'd be curious to watch them.
They're asleep, though, far too busy
doing smile-shots, boot-shots, raised-arm-shots.
Him and him and her they leave to their dreaming.

This one, startled at 3 a.m. to breathless
alert, can't doze. How can he dream
sweetly? Even here where he's fled to,
their broadly tormenting smile comes up the street
towards him. He goes the long way round
these days or darts into sleep and dreams
suddenly, when there's nobody there.

LOCKED

You can forgive, you say,
the man who beat your feet,
who hung you up by your hands,
who drove you past pain's limit.

The man you can't forgive
tortured next door, next cell:
beat your friend, hung your friend
by the hands, made your friend howl.

Your cries lay down with you,
touching, coaxing, whispering.
Your friend's cries are locked
in the cell of your hearing.

ASYLUM

It's one in the morning here
and five where he lies sleeping.
Her feet howl as he beats her.

Whatever was done, keeps.
It's one in the morning here
and five where he lies sleeping.

THE BURNING HOUSE

1. Case

On the map of your case for asylum
there's a small hole in the page
where your home-village was.

Then there's your first arrest.
Holes are deeper here, more jagged:
they made you strip, they assaulted you.

After that there's a gap: three
empty years when you looked after cows
and the flesh is whole, unopened.

From there a broken bottle
has printed the route you took on your thigh:
Darfur, Khartoum, London.

2. Visitors

'You'd be surprised, sir.'
The guard of your prison in England
has seen all sorts. 'Gentleman came last week,
had this substance secreted.
Used every crevice he'd got, sir.'

His fingers flicker over us.
Even he is dumbfounded
by what he finds: that we
tried to smuggle our outrage
past his amiability.

We can have it back when we go.
Now, though, when we come on you
in your prison bib at a table,
all we've brought is the dead
weight of advantage.

3. During sun and rain

Your long sky ended here,
deep in the midlands of England.

Asylum's a green wind
that sings in Her Majesty's corridor.

You clap big farmer's hands
silently together.

4. Shepherd's Bush

Where (absurdly) was this
phone-box where you used to sleep
in the angry London winter?
You raise wide smiling eyes.
I think you kept cows not sheep

on the land they stole.
Now, though, when we break
the latest news from Western Sudan,
you rock forward and hold
your poor hurt lamb

in your arms. You can't say
home any longer, or children,
or wife. Politely you scour
our city. A desolate place
to keep sheep is what you're searching for.

5. In the telling

When words fail
or the voice fails words
that need to be said and accepted,
your left hand goes on speaking,

flicking open and closed
as though you're not so much scattering
grain as throwing it away
on land you've had to abandon.

Your voice can't say what was done,
what the young men did when they came.
Atrocity you have to say
left-handed.

6. The burning house

As though this
was the morning after,
we visit you in prison and view
the burning house of you.

Janjaweed keep coming:
blackening the houses, then,
when you're building back,
bristling round you and cramming you

over and over
into the back of their car,
hilarious even now your gasp
when they stub your flesh with burn-holes.

Bad sleeping, you say.
Smoke grieves in the timbers,
breathes from the black of the house.
Startles back into fire.

7. Seventeen five

On 17.5.02 I must have just
bought my bicycle
and you, for the second time,
were arrested and taken away.

For seventeen days I was riding
through England while you were in prison
in Darfur. Now I know that,
all my strenuous pedalling
turns out to have been free-wheeling.

Upside-down,
wheels on the loose in the air,
bicycles go both ways.
To pray is to kneel by the chain
and turn back the pedals by hand.

I'm not asking
for seventeen days of torture
to be uncycled.
Two years six months of you
remembering things they did to you,
that's what I want pedalled back.

8. Snarl

"Didn't even look, did ya?"
Best of British,
a scratched white van
stops in traffic next to me.

It's true, I didn't look.
I took a chance and came.
Plus I'm cycling away
between and through and ahead.

Connoisseur of resentment,
what about you? Didn't look
either, did you? Fled
like me and utterly

unlike me: you
who have known a broken
bottle's resentment
of human flesh.

9. Next to the lorries

I take the long way round,
use words, go clockwise
round M25, avoid London.

Not like the hoarse roar
of your fatherliness
when it hears the news from Darfur.

In the queue at Dartford Crossing
I'm nothing next to the lorries.
You grow huge with your losing.